Open the Door to Liberty!

Open the Door to Liberty!

A BIOGRAPHY OF
TOUSSAINT L'OUVERTURE

By Anne Rockwell

Illustrated by R. Gregory Christie

HOUGHTON MIFFLIN BOOKS FOR CHILDREN
HOUGHTON MIFFLIN HARCOURT
BOSTON 2009

Houghton Mifflin Books for Children is an imprint of
Houghton Mifflin Harcourt Publishing Company.

www.hmhbooks.com

The text of this book is set in Fournier.
The illustrations are gouache on Strathmore illustration board.

Library of Congress Cataloging-in-Publication Data
Rockwell, Anne.
Open the door to liberty! : a biography of Toussaint L'Ouverture /
by Anne Rockwell ; illustrated by R. Gregory Christie.
p. cm.
ISBN 978-0-618-60570-5
1. Toussaint Louverture, 1743?–1803—Juvenile literature. 2. Haiti—
History—Revolution, 1791–1804—Juvenile literature. 3. Revolutionaries—
Haiti—Biography—Juvenile literature. 4. Generals—Haiti—Biography—
Juvenile literature. I. Christie, Gregory, 1971–. II. Title.
F1923.T69R63 2007
972.94'03092—dc22
[B] 2007025746

Printed in China
WKT 10 9 8 7 6 5 4 3 2 1

For Eveline
— A.R.

For Martine and Angie
— R.G.C.

Preface

*M*any brave and remarkable people came before us. Those who helped us become the best we can be should never be forgotten. One such hero was a black man with a French name who was born a slave on an island in the Caribbean Sea. We don't hear much about him today, but what he did changed his world and ours. He opened the door to liberty for black people everywhere. His actions helped make the United States the world power it is today.

This is his story.

Little Stick

In about 1743 a skinny, puny baby boy was born on the island of St. Domingue in the Caribbean Sea. Both his parents were slaves who'd been born in West Africa. Before their baby was born they had consulted a wise woman, an African-born slave who knew how to communicate with the powerful spirit world. She predicted that their son would be very special. She said he would grow up to be more than a man. He would be a nation.

As with all messages from the spirits, the meaning of this one was not entirely clear. And when the baby was born, it seemed as though the wise woman's prediction was wrong. Everyone was sure he would die soon after he was born. But that baby boy arrived with great determination. He fought for life, and won. He hung in day after day until he was christened Francois-Dominique Toussaint Breda. No birth records were kept for slaves, but his birthday may

have been November 1, since that is All Saints Day, or *La Toussaint* in French. His name was French because his island was a colony of France. His last name was Breda after the plantation where he was born.

Although his parents called him Toussaint, the other slave children nicknamed him "Little Stick." That's because he was as skinny as the thinnest branches of the ebony trees that grew on the fertile island.

Toussaint didn't want to be called "Little Stick." He wanted to be as strong as a great tree. Every day he swam across rivers and rode horseback until he was exhausted, and every day he rode and swam farther than he had the day before. He never did get very tall, but he did get mighty strong.

He was also a quiet and mysterious child who everyone believed was deep and wise. He liked to seek out quiet places where he could be alone with his thoughts.

Gaou-Guinou, his father, was a prince of the Aradas tribe and had been captured in war, sold into slavery, then brought to St.

Domingue. His master treated him differently from most slaves because of his noble manner. He and his wife, Pauline, lived near the Breda plantation on their own land—and led a life little different from those of free people.

Their first son was also more fortunate than most slave children. Toussaint was never whipped or mistreated. He lived with his parents and his seven younger brothers and sisters on a comfortable farm. He had a godfather who was a freed slave, a man named Pierre Baptiste Simon. Baptiste had learned to read from Catholic priests and in turn taught Toussaint, for he recognized how remarkably intelligent this child was.

Even so, Toussaint knew the cruelty that other slaves suffered. He saw slave ships in the harbor unloading their chained and brutalized human cargo. He saw what happened when slaves dared to revolt.

In 1759, when Toussaint was about sixteen years old, a man named François Mackandal did rebel. He was one of a group of people called Maroons (which comes from the word *cimarron*, meaning "wild" in Spanish). Maroons were slaves who ran away repeatedly, who refused to work no matter how badly they were beaten, who would sooner die than live as slaves. Their owners often gave up and let them be as long as they stayed away from the other slaves and didn't cause trouble. They lived behind tall fences in isolated villages high in the mountains.

But Mackandal broke the rules Maroons were supposed to live by. Late at night he visited plantations and persuaded slaves to join him in his plan of poisoning the masters, then seizing power over the plantations. By day he mixed kettles of poison in a secret cave. He distributed packets of the dried and powdered poison to his followers in the dead of night. His followers slipped it into the soup bowls or wineglasses of their masters and mistresses.

About six thousand white plantation owners and managers died before any white person found out about Mackandal's plot. Finally one of his followers was tortured until he talked. Mackandal was taken prisoner and brought to the main square in the island's largest city, Le Cap, where he was burned at the stake in front of crowds of slaves. One was Toussaint.

He watched flames destroy Mackandal. Other slaves insisted their hero was not dead but had flown away in the form of a mosquito.

They believed he would come again.

Meanwhile, the young Toussaint was allowed to read any books he wanted in the library of the big house. One was by Julius Caesar, the Roman general who'd conquered a neighboring people called the Gauls. Toussaint learned that there had been slaves in Rome. They hadn't come from Africa, and they weren't black. He then understood that slavery wasn't simply a matter of color. White people could be slaves, too. One of those long-ago Roman slaves, named Spartacus, had led a rebellion against the great Roman army—a rebellion that had come close to victory.

In time the descendants of warring Romans and Gauls made peace and became France, the nation that ruled St. Domingue. Toussaint read books by French philosophers who wrote of the goodness, strength, and love of liberty shared by all human beings. One book, by a priest named Abbot Raynal, told the history of the West Indies, where Toussaint was born. Raynal believed in liberty for all human beings, whatever their color. He predicted that one day a leader would rise up from slavery in one of those Caribbean islands to lead his wretched people to freedom.

Toussaint began to dream that he was destined to be the leader Raynal foretold. But, being Toussaint, who always kept his thoughts to himself, he told no one.

The Tree Grows

Gaou-Guinou had been a healer in his native land. He taught his oldest son how to use plants to heal wounds and cure illnesses, and how to perform surgery. Toussaint's years of strengthening himself on horseback taught him to understand and communicate with those beautiful animals, to know when they were sick and needed care. So he worked at healing horses as well as people.

When he was a young man, his master, Bayon de Libertad, put him in charge of all the animals on the Breda plantation. This was an important position—one that normally wouldn't be entrusted to a slave. Toussaint was also Bayon de Libertad's coachman. He learned the geography of St. Domingue on long rides over the green, mountainous island's roads and paths. He liked to draw and figured out how to draw maps of the island. There seemed little that Toussaint Breda couldn't figure out.

When he was about thirty-three, his master set him free. That put him in the elite company of about thirty thousand free people of color, most of whom were "mulat," with one white parent or grandparent. Only a few free people were of pure African descent like Toussaint. Free blacks and mulattos didn't have the rights that the twenty-five thousand whites of St. Domingue did, but almost. Their situation was wonderful compared to that of the half million black slaves who worked on the sugar plantations.

Most of these people had been born in Africa. They suffered beatings, burnings, and other unspeakable tortures. Few babies were born to slave women, and of those few many died. But the work had to go on. So many slaves died each year that new ones were brought across the sea from Africa regularly.

Toussaint was a small and homely man, but he was gracious and charming. Women adored him. He had many girlfriends, but when

he was near forty he decided it was time to settle down. He married a woman named Suzan Simon, a relative of his godfather, Baptiste. She already had a small son named Placide, whom Toussaint adopted. Placide soon had a brother named Isaac, and another named St. Jean. Later Toussaint and Suzan adopted a little homeless orphan girl named Rose.

They worked a small coffee farm together and prospered. They did so well that they always had food to share with hungry slaves, who were welcome at their cooking fire.

Toussaint didn't know how quickly his life would change. The eighteenth century was a time when many people who had been denied their rights were rising up to claim them. English-speaking colonists on the continent of North America fought for their freedom in 1776 against the king of England, and won.

Another uprising took place in 1789 in France. People who had no land, no money, and no rights demanded food and rights. They weren't slaves, and they weren't black, but they worked for rich and greedy people who didn't pay them enough to eat. Throngs of these ragged, hungry working people marched through the streets of Paris carrying pitchforks and knives, broomsticks and torches, demanding three things—"Liberty! Equality! Brotherhood!"

The king and queen of France were forced from their thrones and executed. A revolutionary government was set up. News traveled slowly in those days, but even so, word of this uprising reached St. Domingue when a ship from France sailed into Le Cap two months later. A sailor shouted through the streets of the city, broadcasting the amazing news of what had happened in Paris in the name of "Liberty! Equality! Brotherhood!"

Those three words moved Toussaint to tears. Yes—he agreed. People everywhere should have liberty, equality, and brotherhood— black or white, man, woman, or child.

In 1791 there was another slave uprising on St. Domingue. This time fifty thousand slaves revolted under the leadership of a slave named Boukman Dutty. Boukman was a man of great intelligence and charisma. He had been born in Jamaica but sold in St. Domingue. While in English-speaking Jamaica he was called Book Man because he loved to read. He was also huge, and awesome to behold. He had lost one hand in an accident in a sugar mill, but he managed well without it. He was a voodoo priest, or houngan.

Toussaint, like his godfather, Baptiste, was a devout Catholic, but voodoo was the religion of most slaves. Its worshipers prayed and made offerings to spirits they had worshiped in Africa, in combination with certain Christian saints with similar qualities to the African "loas," or spirits.

Under Boukman's orders, slaves grabbed machetes, pitchforks, and torches to fight the French soldiers who'd been ordered by the governor of the island to put down the revolt. Some of the slaves made armor for themselves by tying mattresses around their bare chests to protect themselves from French gunfire and swords. Many died, including Boukman himself. But even without him the fighting went on.

Toussaint packed up his medical supplies, mounted his horse, and galloped up to the mountains to care for the wounded. When he saw how determined these slaves were, he knew his time had come, the time Raynal had written of. The slaves were brave but disorganized. They needed a leader. So even though he was forty-eight years old, gray-haired, and free, Toussaint joined them. Most slaves didn't live to be as old as Toussaint. His followers called him "Old Toussaint," but they listened to what he had to say. His voice was magnificent. It carried far, and his words were moving and eloquent.

He returned home for a short time to send his wife and children to a cottage safely hidden in the woods. He also told Bayon de Libertad that he and his wife must leave St. Domingue before they were killed. His former master and mistress stepped into the carriage for a last ride through the island's lush green forests. Toussaint drove them to a ship sailing for Baltimore in the United States. Then he raced back to the bloody sugar cane fields.

With him as leader the battle turned and the French soldiers retreated. Those slaves without clothes or shoes or horses or swords saw how this small gray-haired man could fight as long and hard as the youngest and strongest of them. He was as strong as a tree, just as he'd made up his mind to be when he was called "Little Stick." He could always see an opening to victory. Soon he wasn't called "Old Toussaint" but "L'Ouverture," which in French means "the opening."

The Soldier

In 1793 the revolutionary government in Paris paid attention to what had happened in St. Domingue. A law was passed decreeing that slaves in all French colonies were free.

It was miraculous! Toussaint L'Ouverture had led the first triumphant slave rebellion in history. Word spread throughout the Caribbean islands, the United States, and Europe. Slaves who heard the news were thrilled by what Toussaint had done, and those who owned slaves were frightened.

The French Revolution and its motto of "Liberty, Equality, and Brotherhood!" also frightened all the major powers in Europe. Royal leaders and aristocrats believed its message of liberty and equality for all spelled their doom, just as it had for the royalty and nobility of France. The powerful nations of Great Britain and Spain decided to take advantage of the postrevolution disorder in France and try to capture its wealthy colony of St. Domingue.

Then Toussaint and his army proved their value to France. They fought victoriously for France against Britain, then Spain, when those powers tried to take the island. The army Toussaint had trained and led was made up of black, mulatto, and white soldiers. He gained seven victories in seven days. France appointed him governor-general of St. Domingue.

It was time to rebuild the island. Now all the people of St. Domingue had to act as one for the good of all.

For those former slaves who didn't believe they could ever live as equals with their despised former masters, Toussaint had an answer. He'd fill a bottle with many black seeds, and fewer white ones, then shake it until all the seeds were mixed together to show what he

meant by one people. He didn't want those who'd been slaves to take revenge on their former masters, even though most had been treated monstrously. Revenge gained nothing, he was convinced. It would bring only more fighting, death, and destruction. Now fields had to be replanted. Towns and roads had to be rebuilt. Children had to be cared for. Toussaint was a mystery to most adults, serious and aloof with them, but he loved children. He laughed and cried with them, and he couldn't bear to see them hungry or alone. He also saw what his education had enabled him to understand and do and wanted all children to have such an opportunity.

Many people who'd been born in Africa resented having to work in sugar fields now that they were free. They remembered life in Africa and wanted the same in St. Domingue. That meant working in small fields outside small villages, growing just what they needed for their family and perhaps a little extra to sell in the market—no more.

Toussaint understood that his people were changed forever. With liberty came the responsibilities of free people. To succeed, the land had to be prosperous. Toussaint understood this, but he had to convince others. And they couldn't spend a lot of time arguing about it. The land had been ravaged by war. Not only plantations but also the small gardens of free people and slaves had been burned to ashes. If the people Toussaint now led didn't work hard, they would become victims of stronger powers. They couldn't go back to what they had been across the sea, though their hearts might still be there.

They needed money to send bright teenagers to school in Paris so they could return to St. Domingue as teachers of the island's younger children. Toussaint and Suzan set an example by sending their oldest sons, Placide and Isaac, to Paris to be educated. The

island needed engineers to keep roads in repair, to keep the irrigation canals French engineers had built flowing. The island needed the skills of the white people who hadn't run away or been killed in the uprising.

St. Domingue had riches to trade. In spite of all the fighting, it was still the richest island in the Caribbean. Toussaint believed its people had to go on growing and selling sugar, coffee, cotton, and tobacco to Europe and the United States—particularly the United States. If they didn't, they would starve in isolation from the world. They needed to work as hard as when they'd been slaves. But now the profits from their work would be for their needs, not those of greedy masters.

What the wise woman had foretold at his birth had come true.

Toussaint had become more than a man. He was the leader of a people whose history and destiny were unique in the world. He and his followers had become a new people—a world-shaking nation.

Many people listened to Toussaint's great and eloquent voice and did what he said. But others resented his orders. As was his way, Toussaint never discussed his plans. He thought—then acted. He had many horses stabled all over the island, and people got used to his abruptly leaving a meeting, mounting a horse, and galloping off with no explanation. No one knew when or where he might suddenly appear. As soon as he arrived at a stable where he had another horse, he exchanged the exhausted one for the fresh one and continued on his way. People kept busy—just in case he arrived when they were taking it easy. And St. Domingue healed and prospered.

Governing more than half a million people was different from being in charge of the livestock of one plantation. Since St. Domingue was a French colony, letters had to be written and sent to the government in Paris by ship. Toussaint could read French, but he couldn't speak or write it well. His spoken language was Creole, a combination of French, Spanish, English, and various African languages. Since slave traders never filled a ship with many people from the same tribe, who could communicate with one another and plot against them, slaves invented a language common to them all.

But Toussaint couldn't write letters in Creole to French people in Paris. They wouldn't be able to read them. So he had five secretaries who could speak, read, and write both French and Creole. One was

always at his side carrying paper, ink, and a quill pen. Toussaint dictated what he wanted to say in Creole, then listened as the secretary translated and read it back to him in French. He edited the words until they were exactly as he wished them to be. Only then would he sign his name with his bold scrawl. He always misspelled it, however, leaving out the apostrophe that in French should be between L and O.

His plans, however secretly and mysteriously he arrived at them, went well. There was something about Toussaint that made him seem born to command—something rare and magical that everyone noticed.

The second president of the United States, John Adams, admired Toussaint L'Ouverture and encouraged Americans to trade with him. Toussaint was very interested in these people who'd also revolted against tyranny. He liked to stop at the elegant hotel he'd built in Le Cap and talk with American guests. He was often accompanied by one of his generals, Henry Christophe, who had been born on St. Kitts, a British island, and spoke English and French well. Christophe was a sophisticated man of the world who had been a cabin boy on a French ship and traveled far. As a twelve-year-old he'd served as a drummer boy in Georgia with French troops that came to help General George Washington in the American War of Independence.

American visitors couldn't believe that this small, quiet man with gracious manners was really Toussaint L'Ouverture, the famous and fearsome black warrior. But as they looked into his eyes they decided there was indeed something extraordinary about him—even something frightening. His face was as black and still as an

African mask, revealing nothing of what he was thinking, but his eyes seemed to stare right into one's soul and know what was hidden there.

Toussaint had trained another man named Jean-Jacques Dessalines to be one of his most powerful generals. Although he couldn't read or write, Dessalines devised very smart battle plans. He was a brave and brilliant soldier, but he was filled with hate. People called him "The Tiger"—not just because of his fierceness in battle but because his body was as ringed with stripes as a tiger's. Those raised stripes were scars from the many whippings he'd had when he was a slave.

After a victory, Toussaint always gave the order, "No reprisals! No reprisals!" He hated any more killing than was necessary in battle, especially the killing of women and children—black, white, or brown. Whenever Dessalines heard this order he fidgeted in angry frustration with his proudest possession, an elegant French gold enameled snuffbox. He wanted to avenge himself on all whites and mulats remaining on St. Domingue. But his wife agreed with Toussaint, and Dessalines adored her. Between the two of them, he obeyed.

Men of Destiny

By the year 1800 the United States had elected its third president, Thomas Jefferson. France claimed as a colony the port city of New Orleans, where the Mississippi River empties into the Gulf of Mexico. This troubled Jefferson. There were few roads in the new nation, and goods were moved up and down the huge river by boat. What if France decided to deny access to the river? If the United States owned New Orleans, the river would be forever safe and free of French control. Jefferson asked his ambassador to France to open up negotiations to purchase New Orleans. But it didn't happen.

Just as Toussaint L'Ouverture was the strong leader his people needed, an equally strong leader had risen out of the chaos of revolutionary France. Napoleon Bonaparte was a brilliant, ambitious, and charismatic young general who seized power to become first consul of the French Republic. He ruled with more power than the king ever had and didn't hesitate to go to war against European rulers who opposed him. Like Toussaint, Napoleon inspired awe in all who met him, whether they admired or despised him.

The two were alike in other ways. Napoleon, too, was smaller than most men. Like Toussaint, he loved to read. Both had been noted for their remarkable intelligence as children. Napoleon had been born in Corsica, which had been part of Italy until shortly after his birth. Like Toussaint, he never spoke French as well as he would have wished, for he hadn't learned the language until he was ten years old. He had a strong Italian accent and misspelled many French words. Both men had incredible energy—working hard, eating and sleeping little. Both were fearless. People believed that great forces must have been watching over each of them, for neither was ever seriously

wounded. Napoleon's soldiers adored him, for like Toussaint he fought, ate, and slept alongside them—never asking them to do something he wouldn't do. He rewarded them with promotions for courage and talent, not for wealth or aristocratic birth.

Like Toussaint, the first consul always kept his ideas to himself until he was ready to act.

In one way, though, the two were very different. Whereas Toussaint was the finest horseman ever seen in his part of the world, even Napoleon's admirers joked behind his back that he bounced along on his horse like a sack of potatoes slung across a donkey.

Like Toussaint L'Ouverture, Napoleon Bonaparte was always referred to by his first name. And Napoleon believed, as did Toussaint, that he was born to change the world. He was called the "Man of Destiny."

Some people, especially black people who were slaves on other Caribbean islands and in the United States, said Toussaint was their own "Man of Destiny."

Napoleon's wife, Josephine, who'd been born on the island of Martinique in the French Caribbean, joked to her husband that he was becoming the Toussaint L'Ouverture of Europe.

Napoleon was furious. Napoleon had a lot of racial prejudice, so for him it was bad enough that his wife's family included a mulatto brother-in-law. There was only one Napoleon! No one had his genius—especially not a former black slave. He had his own plans for St. Domingue, and they were very different from Toussaint's.

A Cruel Secret

France needed money as much as St. Domingue did. Years of revolution and war had impoverished the nation. Napoleon wanted the greater profits of slave-grown sugar and secretly planned to restore slavery in all the French West Indian islands, including St. Domingue. Then he intended to launch a conquest of the land France claimed on the North American continent.

No one knew of this except General Charles Victor-Emmanuel LeClerc. The brave and handsome husband of Napoleon's favorite sister, Pauline, was given the job of carrying out the first stage of the plan. In a long secret document to LeClerc, Napoleon gave orders that Toussaint was to be gotten rid of, and he wrote instructions as to how it should be done.

LeClerc should flatter him at first. As soon as he had Toussaint's trust, he was to take him prisoner and ship him to France.

Perhaps Napoleon, with his huge ego, overestimated Toussaint's own influence, not acknowledging how much the black people of St. Domingue would do for liberty, with or without their leader.

Napoleon was confident that after Toussaint was gone slavery would be easily restored by force. LeClerc and his troops (including those black soldiers and officers trained by Toussaint) would then sail for New Orleans to occupy the great unmapped land west of the Mississippi River, the land called the Louisiana Territory, which France claimed.

When LeClerc sailed from France, more than twenty thousand soldiers followed in many ships. It was a huge military undertaking. Napoleon's army was the bravest and best trained in Europe. Some weren't French but freelance mercenary soldiers from various nations who made their living going to war for whatever country paid them. A few of these mercenaries were American.

At the beginning of 1801, Toussaint stood at the crest of a hill near Le Cap overlooking the sea. It was a place where he liked to go to think. When he saw the huge fleet sailing toward the island, he guessed immediately why they had come. He was horrified that the first consul, whom he had up to that moment admired and trusted, would set out to destroy the very liberty he claimed to believe in. But Toussaint could see no other reason that Napoleon had sent such a large fleet.

Thomas Jefferson also learned of the massive fleet sailing to St. Domingue. Why had Napoleon sent so many soldiers? St. Domingue was at peace. Jefferson rightly suspected that the troops planned to continue on to the United States, which wouldn't stand a

chance against this invasion. It had an army of fewer than one thousand men.

In those days conquering armies lived by occupying the homes and eating the food of the conquered. Toussaint knew his people could survive off the land better than Europeans could, for it was their home. The French soldiers would have a difficult time managing without cities and towns and farms to feed and house them. So Toussaint, Dessalines, and Christophe made plans for the island's defense. They would each be in charge of one-third of the island,

and they would burn everything the French could eat or sleep in as the army advanced.

Henry Christophe had the job of defending Le Cap. Shortly before the first French troops came ashore, Christophe gave his orders. He began by putting a torch to the curtains in his own elegant home. Citizens ran screaming through the streets toward the mountains as the fire spread and an ammunition warehouse exploded. General LeClerc and his soldiers came ashore to nothing but ashes.

The war that Napoleon had assured LeClerc would take only a month had begun.

LeClerc saw immediately that Napoleon had been overly optimistic. The first consul didn't know what expert fighters these soldiers and officers Toussaint L'Ouverture had trained were. They were also well equipped with American-made cannons, uniforms, and guns.

Hidden in the mountain forests, Toussaint's soldiers attacked without warning. More and more of LeClerc's army fell. He wrote Napoleon, begging him to come and see for himself how courageous and undefeatable these black soldiers were. He told the first consul how well disciplined these former slaves were, and, most important, how willing they were to die for liberty, having tasted its sweetness.

Toussaint also wrote Napoleon. He begged him to come and see the beautiful island he had governed so well for France, assuring him that they could work together for the same great cause—liberty and peace for all.

But Napoleon didn't answer Toussaint's letters; so Toussaint sent messages to his generals, saying "Wait until the rains come."

Mackandal's Return?

In the tropics there are two seasons, wet and dry. Starting in March, rain comes down hard every day, as it always does in that season, year after year. It leaves puddles, where dormant mosquito eggs hatch.

In Toussaint's time no one knew that a certain mosquito's sting caused one of the most dangerous diseases of the tropics. But he and many others must have noticed that black people didn't catch it as readily or as severely as whites. Yellow fever may have come from Africa in stagnant pools of water on the slave ships. People from Africa had generations of exposure to the virus that causes yellow fever, immunity Europeans lacked. The disease attacks the liver and causes the skin and whites of the eyes to turn yellow with jaundice before the victim dies. The slaves who'd prophesied that the spirit of Mackandal lived on in the form of a mosquito were close to the truth. With the rains, yellow fever began attacking the French troops.

One of the mercenary soldiers serving under LeClerc was from Kentucky. He struck up a conversation with an American business-man he met in Le Cap, telling him he'd be glad to get home. It wouldn't be long, he confided. LeClerc would be continuing on to New Orleans as soon as they were finished on St. Domingue.

Spies brought this news to Jefferson.

More than twenty thousand soldiers had come to a strange land to fight under General LeClerc. Many of these young Europeans believed that it was a far better fate to be conquered by Napoleon, to serve in his army, than to be ruled and kept subservient by their nobility.

England was the strongest enemy Napoleon had. The party line of Napoleon's followers was that just as the American colonists had fought to rid themselves of British rule, so must all Caribbean islands defend themselves against Britain. Soldiers fighting under LeClerc in St. Domingue believed what they were told—that Toussaint was an enemy of France who was planning to bargain away the riches of that island to British colonial forces in nearby Jamaica.

It didn't matter whether these European soldiers were French or not. After all, their hero wasn't French by birth!

The truth was the opposite of what they thought. Indeed, Britain was a threat. That nation had tried to take advantage of France after the successful slave rebellion led by Toussaint L'Ouverture. But European soldiers in Napoleon's great army, many of whom spoke neither English nor French, had no way of knowing that Toussaint had been a hero for France when he drove English and Spanish would-be conquerors out of St. Domingue and saved the island for France.

They believed they were fighting against English tyranny that would destroy liberty wherever it found it. Hadn't France come to the aid of the American colonists in their War of Independence, their war for their liberty against the king of England? Soldiers were willing to die for the great cause of liberty, for it was their cause too.

But things happened to make them question the war's purpose.

One night twelve thousand of LeClerc's soldiers pitched their tents outside the walls of a fort where Dessalines had stationed twelve hundred soldiers. Suddenly they heard singing from behind the walls. They recognized the words and music immediately.

Come—children of the homeland!
Our day of glory has arrived!
Let us fight against all tyranny
That flies its bloody flag!

How could this be? The black soldiers inside the fort were singing the very song that the poor of Paris had sung years earlier as they marched through the streets! They knew it well, for the stirring "Marseillaise" had become the national anthem of the French Republic.

Was it possible that the first consul had deceived them? Was it possible that they had been sent to St. Domingue not to preserve liberty but to destroy it?

One entire regiment, which happened to be made up of Polish soldiers, decided that this was indeed the case. That night they surrendered. When morning came the regiment fought with, not against, Dessalines and his soldiers.

In spite of this event, Dessalines was still convinced that there could be no peace between black and white people—that St. Domingue must win independence from France, kill all the whites on the island, and go its own way.

But Toussaint did not agree.

Surprise and Betrayal

Yellow fever was spreading fast among the French troops. Napoleon ordered reinforcements to St. Domingue—another thirty thousand troops under the command of General Donatien-Marie-Joseph de Vimeur, vicomte de Rochambeau.

To everyone's surprise, Christophe suddenly surrendered to the French. LeClerc tried to bribe him to turn Toussaint over, knowing that Christophe liked to live extravagantly. To his credit, Christophe refused.

If Toussaint, who left a record of who he was in the many eloquent letters he wrote to various members of the government in Paris, is an enigma, Christophe is more of one. Some historians believe he was severely mentally ill, with violent mood swings that went from full of grandiose ideas to deep despair. He seems to have been a man of charm and charisma whom Toussaint found useful.

Was it a plot of his that Christophe should surrender when he did? And if so, why?

Historians don't understand why Christophe surrendered or what happened next. French soldiers were dying in great numbers each day, and LeClerc himself was sick with yellow fever. Toussaint had the advantage. But since he never shared his thoughts with others, no one knows to this day why Toussaint did what he did.

He sent word that he wanted to meet with LeClerc and work out terms for his surrender. It's possible that Toussaint, a wily politician who understood human nature, wanted to let LeClerc, and through him, the first consul, save face. If Napoleon and the French people believed they had been victorious, in spite of their terrible losses, Napoleon would retain power. Toussaint may have been gambling that it was better to deal with the enemy he knew than the unknown. Or he may have simply believed that there had been too much fighting and dying, too much destruction of the beautiful forests and farms in the land he was so proud of. It was time for peace, time to rebuild. Because he had the advantage, with his great self-confidence Toussaint may have been sure he could control peace from behind the scenes. In peace, and seemingly without power, he would work with Napoleon for the good of France and St. Domingue, and for liberty everywhere.

But he didn't understand how much Napoleon hated him, although the two men had never met.

General Toussaint L'Ouverture rode to town wearing his full dress uniform with golden epaulettes, shining boots, three-cornered hat, and gleaming sword, for he knew this was a solemn moment for him and his country. The road was lined for miles with people toss-

ing flowers in his path, calling out, "Papa Toussaint! Never leave us!"

Toussaint promised he wouldn't.

He offered to retire from active duty and tend to his farm. In return for this offer of peace he wanted assurance that slavery would never be restored on St. Domingue, that all soldiers and officers in his army could stay armed, even though he himself would not be. LeClerc agreed to the terms and Toussaint returned home.

Then Dessalines surrendered. He was shrewd. Dessalines knew that most of the French soldiers were dead or dying. LeClerc would join them, he was sure. But as long as Napoleon's brother-in-law was around and in power, Dessalines would play the white man's game.

He swore allegiance to LeClerc and told him he could always trust and rely on him. As he did, Dessalines warned LeClerc that although

he himself could be trusted, LeClerc must never trust Toussaint. It wasn't true, but Dessalines knew he would soon rule, and rule according to his own bitter and brutal convictions, not Toussaint's far more humane vision.

Even though Dessalines betrayed Toussaint, he was not the cause of what happened next. Napoleon had already decided Toussaint's fate.

One of LeClerc's officers invited Toussaint to dinner to discuss further details of the peace treaty. When Toussaint entered the dining room, French soldiers jumped him and tied him up. They took him to a ship sailing that night for France. His last words as he boarded it were, "You have cut down the trunk of the tree of liberty, but the roots will push on, for they are many and deep!"

A Cold Country

When the ship reached France, Toussaint was led to a carriage. Its windows were covered with black curtains. The carriage with its prisoner sped across France until it came to a toll road. Soldiers on guard demanded that the door be opened before it could pass.

Several of them had fought under General Toussaint L'Ouverture when he drove the English from St. Domingue. They recognized their former commanding officer. Each of them saluted him, their eyes glistening. Toussaint solemnly returned the salute. Then the door closed and the carriage continued on its way.

When it reached an ancient fortress in the mountains near the Swiss border, called the Fort de Joux, Toussaint was led to a chilly, dismal room where water dripped constantly from the vaulted stone ceiling onto the cold stone floor. In this part of France, surrounded by snow, rain, mist, and fog, the sun rarely shone. Not that it mattered. The one small window in his cell was too far up to see anything but endless gray clouds.

There was a fireplace with a chair, where Toussaint sat shivering, his teeth chattering. Each day an interrogator sent by Napoleon visited, insisting Toussaint tell him where he had hidden treasure he'd stolen and what secrets he had sold to the English.

But Toussaint had no treasure and had never sold secrets.

He managed to write Napoleon, begging for a trial where he could see what evidence there was against him. But no answer came. The great and broken-hearted Toussaint L'Ouverture soon died in his cold, damp prison.

The Tiger

The roots of the tree of liberty planted on the island of St. Domingue did indeed push on, but not without much more bloodshed. Thirty thousand French troops reached St. Domingue under the command of General de Rochambeau. LeClerc died of yellow fever, and Rochambeau began a massacre of black civilians that was far more brutal than anything LeClerc had ordered.

These atrocities, the murders of women and children and old people, proved to Dessalines what he had always believed—that whites could never be trusted. His surrender and pledge of loyalty had, after all, been to LeClerc, who was dead, not to Rochambeau. So he began to fight again. Dessalines and his men returned atrocity for atrocity, killing all whites and mulats they found.

Every day newspapers in the United States carried news of the bloody massacres in St. Domingue, especially those committed by

Dessalines. American businessmen were afraid to go to St. Domingue to trade.

French losses under Rochambeau were as great as those under LeClerc. The yellow fever epidemic continued to spread among the new French troops. Dessalines gave orders that every white person on St. Domingue should be shot, hanged, burned, or taken offshore and drowned.

Napoleon considered the terrible news and decided that the war on St. Domingue wasn't worth fighting. He was determined now to invade England, yet had lost most of his finest fighting men on St. Domingue. He'd made an expensive error. Invading Louisiana was also now out of the question. He gave orders for his remaining soldiers to return to France. St. Domingue could have its independence.

Rochambeau surrendered to Dessalines. As soon as he did, he had nowhere to turn except to the British, France's enemy. He surrendered to them, choosing life as a British prisoner of war rather than death under Dessalines. He and fewer than two thousand wounded, exhausted, sick, and dying soldiers, all that was left of the French army in St. Domingue, were taken to England as prisoners of war on British warships.

The remaining civilians boarded commercial vessels and were taken to Jamaica, Cuba, or New Orleans to begin a new life with nothing.

Dessalines had triumphed. He now ruled the devastated but independent island. He ripped the white stripe out of the red, white, and blue flag of the French Republic to make a new flag for the nation he would call Haiti. Long ago, the aboriginal Arawak Indians, who lived

on the island before Columbus discovered it, called it that. The name meant, "Land of the Mountains." Columbus had called it Hispaniola, for Spain, but the French who colonized it later had named it after a saint who they believed looked kindly on them. This saint was St. Domingue.

Dessalines ordered a solid gold crown from goldsmiths in Philadelphia and beautiful velvet robes from England. Since Napoleon was about to be crowned Emperor Napoleon I of France, Dessalines decided he should be crowned Emperor Jacques I of

Haiti. But his rule was short—not much more than a year. Violence ruled. Dessalines was assassinated by followers of Henry Christophe, who crowned himself King Henry I of Haiti. He and a mulatto leader named Andre Petion divided the country into two parts, one part ruled by King Henry I and the other by the more modest Petion.

Christophe's personality became more and more bizarre. His extravagance is lengendary. He built a magnificent palace called Sans Souci, which means "Without a Care," and a mammoth fortress overlooking the harbor in Le Cap, a fortress to defend his terrain from the French, who, in his deepening mistrust of everyone, he was sure would come again.

Even when he was nothing more than a waiter in a hotel, Christophe had loved high living. The parties he threw at Sans Souci were lavish beyond belief—rivaling those of the kings of France who had been overthrown by the hungry and neglected people. People soon forgot about the achievements of the Haitian Revolution, which had been born out of the best ideas of the French Revolution. After six years Christophe, although still young, suffered a stroke and became paralyzed. He fell into a deep depression and committed suicide.

The legacy of greedy French monarchs became Haiti's, and the world judged that young nation by the extravagance and selfishness of Christophe and the brutality of Dessalines—not by the quiet and visionary Toussaint, who died quietly in a cold and miserable prison across the sea.

But he is the one we should remember.

The Prize

The American ambassador to France offered once more to buy the port of New Orleans. This time, Napoleon agreed.

The only condition France made was that the United States buy not only New Orleans but also all the Louisiana Territory. Napoleon needed money so badly that he didn't quibble over the price; he just ordered that payment and paperwork be done quickly. This sale has been called the greatest land bargain in history.

When the Louisiana Territory was ceded to the United States in 1803, no one had any idea how much land there was. Thomas Jefferson's secretary, Meriwether Lewis, and an army officer named William Clark were given the job of organizing a group of twenty-eight men called the "Corps of Discovery" to explore and map the territory. These vast new lands made the United States the huge, wealthy world power it is today.

While American fortunes rose, Napoleon's fell. His huge losses on St. Domingue were the beginning of his end. In 1815 the English Duke of Wellington defeated him at the Belgian town of Waterloo, not far from the French border. Napoleon was taken prisoner by the British and moved to a remote island off the coast of South Africa.

It was a sad and ironic ending for the Man of Destiny. The island of St. Helena was as impossible to escape from as the Fort de Joux, where he'd sent Toussaint to die. As Napoleon reviewed his life and dictated his memoirs, he wondered what would have happened had he worked with Toussaint L'Ouverture rather than wasting so many soldiers in trying to destroy him. He felt this was the greatest mistake he had made in his extraordinary life.

Like Toussaint, Napoleon also died on his island prison.

The Louisiana Purchase changed history. The rich lands and great mineral resources in the West made the United States the most powerful nation in the world. And it came about because of a quiet, brave black man who was inspired by what he read, who came to help the wounded in the sugar cane fields of St. Domingue, and saw openings to a world where liberty ruled.

Cast of Characters

(In order of appearance)

Francois-Dominique Toussaint Breda
(later known as Toussaint L'Ouverture)
Born a slave in St. Domingue about 1743. Set free by his master at the age of thirty-three. Leader of the world's first successful slave revolt. Governor-general of French colony of St. Domingue. Imprisoned in Fort de Joux, France, at Napoleon's orders, where he died.

Gaou-Guinou Breda
Birthdate unknown. Born the son of a chief in the Aradas tribe in West Africa. Captured in battle and sold into slavery. Slave on the Breda plantation in St. Domingue. Father of Toussaint L'Ouverture.

Pauline Breda
Date and place of birth unknown. Wife of Gaou-Guinou and slave on the Breda plantation. Mother of Toussaint L'Ouverture.

Pierre Baptiste Simon
Date and place of birth unknown. Educated Roman Catholic slave. Toussaint's godfather, who saw to it that he learned to read and write.

François Mackandal

Born around 1728 in the Loango Kingdom of West Africa. Maroon leader who plotted to kill all whites on St. Domingue. Captured and burned alive in public in 1758.

Boukman Dutty

Date of birth in Jamaica unknown. Bought and brought to neighboring island of St. Domingue. Voodoo priest (or houngan). Leader of St. Domingue slave revolt in 1791. Killed shortly thereafter in battle.

Henry Christophe

Born in 1767 on the British colony of St. Kitts. Sold to a French sea captain. General on St. Domingue under Toussaint L'Ouverture. Became King Henry (Henri) I of Haiti in 1806. Committed suicide in 1820.

Jean-Jacques Dessalines

Born a slave in St. Domingue in 1758. General under Toussaint L'Ouverture. Became Emperor Jacques I of Haiti in 1805. Killed by followers of Henry Christophe in 1806.

Thomas Jefferson

Born in 1743 in Virginia Colony. Third president of the United States. Author of the Declaration of Independence. Oversaw the Louisiana Purchase by the United States from France in 1803. Dispatched Meriwether Lewis and William Clark to lead an exploration of the lands acquired.

Napoleon Bonaparte

Born in 1769 on the island of Corsica in the Mediterranean Sea, which had just become a territory of France. Successful young general who became first consul of the French Republic in 1799. In 1801 Napoleon ordered the invasion of St. Domingue, the restoration of slavery there, and the capture of Toussaint L'Ouverture.

Charles Victor-Emmanuel LeClerc

Born in 1772 in France. French general sent by his brother-in-law Napoleon in 1802 to invade St. Domingue. Died of yellow fever in St. Domingue in 1802.

Donatien-Marie-Joseph de Vimeur, Vicomte de Rochambeau

Born in 1755 in France. General Donatien Rochambeau replaced General LeClerc in St. Domingue.

Author's Note

It still puzzles me as to why I, a white child growing up in Memphis, Tennessee, would have heard the story of Toussaint L'Ouverture. But I did. I don't remember exactly where I first heard it; it seems like a story I've always known. I never forgot it.

As with many timid children, hero stories thrilled me, and Toussaint's life struck me as a genuine hero story, only not myth or legend but recorded history. It wasn't until I was an adult and found out more about this remarkable man that I discovered what an influence he had been, not only on the island nation of Haiti, but on the United States and the world. When I became an author of books for young readers I thought more children should have a chance to find out about him.

Researching the story involved opening more doors than I had expected, for I discovered that Toussaint's own ideals were strongly intertwined with those of the French Revolution. The racial divisions between blacks and mulats in St. Domingue were also difficult for me, an American, to understand. Going into these matters in greater detail than I have would have required a very long book. What I wanted was simply to share with modern young readers the story of this remarkable man, Toussaint L'Ouverture.

For this reason I have simplified the extremely complicated history of the Haitian Revolution. It isn't acknowledged by many, yet it should be regarded as one of the three most important events in the eighteenth century, the Age of Enlightenment, which could also be called the Age of Revolution. Those events are the American Revolution, the French Revolution, and the Haitian Revolution. We have not yet resolved the many issues these events launched upon the world. For while the French Revolution went further than the American Revolution in its concept of liberty, the Haitian Revolution rightly saw that this concept belonged to all people, not just whites.

Again, in the interest of focusing on Toussaint, I have not gone into the tragic implications of the Louisiana Purchase for the Native American tribes who were inhabitants of that vast territory. I only hope this story will spark the curiosity of its readers so they will go on to learn more about the many openings in the story of Toussaint L'Ouverture.

Author's Sources

Beard, J. R. *Toussaint L'Ouverture: A Biography and Autobiography*, electronic edition. Chapel Hill: Academic Affairs Library, University of North Carolina, 2001. (Originally published in Boston by James Redpath Publisher, 1863.)

Bell, Madison Smartt. *Toussaint Louverture: A Biography*. New York: Pantheon Books, 2007.

Davis, David Brion. *The Problem of Slavery in the Age of Revolution, 1770–1823*. Ithaca, N.Y.: Cornell University Press, 1975.

Fick, Carolyn E. *The Making of Haiti: The Saint Domingue Revolution from Below*. Knoxville: University of Tennessee Press, 1990.

Fleming, Thomas. *The Louisiana Purchase*. Hoboken, N.J.: John Wiley & Sons, 2003.

James, C. L. R. *The Black Jacobins: Toussaint L'Ouverture and the San Domingo Revolution*, second edition, revised. New York: Vintage Books, 1963.

Kastor, Peter J. *The Great Acquisition: An Introduction to the Louisiana Purchase*. Great Falls, Mont.: Lewis & Clark Interpretive Association, 2003.

Korngold, Ralph. *Citizen Toussaint*. Westport, Conn.: Greenwood Press, 1965.

Kurlansky, Mark. *A Continent of Islands: Searching for the Caribbean Destiny*. Cambridge, Mass.: Perseus Publishing, 1992.

Ott, Thomas O. *The Haitian Revolution, 1789–1804*. Knoxville: University of Tennessee Press, 1973.

Rogozinski, Jan. *A Brief History of the Caribbean: From the Arawak and Carib to the Present*, revised edition. New York: Penguin, 2000.